Growing

by Evelyn Bence

Illustrations by Mary Tara O'Keefe

The C.R. Gibson Company
Norwalk, Connecticut

Some mornings
I wake up wondering
who
I will be today.
I lie there
and ask myself:
When will the real me
arrive?

Every day
this same body
gets out of this same bed,
but the inside of my head
seems to change like the light
of the moon,
only I'm
less predictable
than it is.

You might say I'm like
a telephone directory.

Whose number
should I look for
and call up?

The life of the party?
The party pooper?
The leader?
The follower?
The center of the crowd?
The loner?

Sometimes I carefully choose
which page of the directory
I'm going to turn to.
But other times,
the wind blows it open
wherever it wants.
And I just kind of stand back
and watch.

God,
do you have any idea
what I'm talking about?
I mean I'm not illogical
or full of crazy thoughts.
I just feel like Pinnochio
when he said, "Pappa,
I am not sure who I am."

Sometimes I feel
like I'm an adult,
sometimes
like a kid,
sometimes
like one of the gang,
and sometimes
like the odd one out
(sometimes
even on purpose).

When I look through
old photographs,
I think about myself
when I was just a kid.

I can't believe
how little I knew,
but, on the other hand,
I did pretty well
considering
my inexperience.

Each of those years
was a step
on the stairway
up to here.

I wonder who I'd be
if life allowed a person
to run up the stairs
two at a time.

When I'm walking across
the balance beam
without the slightest slip,
I'm the world's best gymnast.
(Who needs to be discovered?)

With a little practice
I can do anything.

Adults
keep asking me
what I'm going to do
when I grow up.

I wonder why
they don't ask me
who I'm going to be?

When I was a kid,
I wanted to grow up
to be just like Mom.
But recently,
I don't know.

Some of her qualities
I don't have,
and some of her choices
wouldn't be mine.

Yet this morning, for a second,
I caught a glimpse of myself
as her, just younger.

It's happened before,
but this time it was scary,
really scary.

Am I she?
Or am I me?

Does my mother think
I'm a new actress
in her old play?
She outgrew the part
so I'm taking her place?

Sometimes she thinks she knows
all my lines.
She forgets
that the story never turns out
the same way twice.

To my father,
I'm like a helium balloon
he's afraid
to let go of.

No, that's not quite right.
To him I'm more like a balloon
not yet full of enough air to fly.

To my grandmother,
I'm a flower garden
tended with love.

To my grandfather,
I'm a good old sport
he wishes had made
the varsity team.

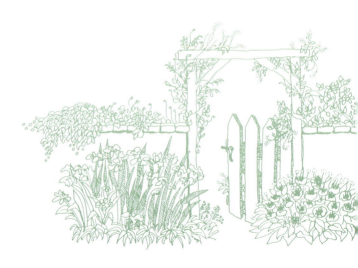

To my best friend,
I'm like a twin sister.

Sometimes we soak ourselves
under running laughter.
Other times
we steady each other
like a rock.

What would I be
if I hadn't found her?
Who knows?

When I'm with my friends,
I'm like a chameleon:
My surroundings determine
my color.

Funny, though,
no matter how I change,
it's always the same I
looking out through
the same set of eyes.

Lord, too often,
no matter how hard I try,
I'm not who I wish I were,
nor who my parents wish I were,
nor, I imagine,
who You wish I were.

Lord, I know You won't give up
on me. Please don't let me give up
on myself. With Your help,
tomorrow will be different—
better—
I promise.

God,
I can't stand
The times I'm left behind,
the times I'm not
let in on the joke,
the times I'm not
invited to the party,
the times I'm not
called for a date.

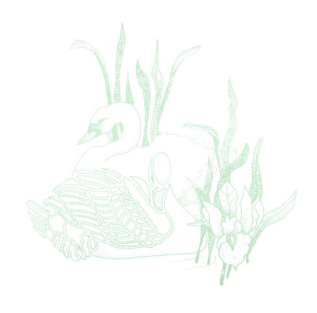

When my name's not on
the in list,
I'm on the outs with myself.

Lord, help me remember
the feeling of those outside days
When I'm on the inside
and tempted to push a friend away.

Last week,
as if a jealous wicked witch
had cast an evil spell on me,
I saw a moonface in my mirror—
hills and craters—
a reflection so marred
I wished I could live in the dark,
turn off the sun,
so no one
could catch a glimpse of me.

But today
my looking glass
tells a tale of wonder:
My eyes, cheeks, nose, smile
are worth a judge's perfect ten.

I'm a woman,
especially when I'm dressed
in my best
and a boy (or is he a man?)
smiles a special smile
at me.

I'm a girl,
especially on Saturdays
when I'm breathing in
the familiar air
of my backyard.

I wonder if
I'll ever,
all the time
feel like a grown-up
and never like a kid.

God,
I hope not.

I wonder
if boys are as unsure
of what I'm thinking
as I am about what
they're thinking.

Imagine!
If one tiny chromosome
had been different,
I would have been born
as "one of them,"
and not "one of us."

I thank you, God
that I'm a girl,
even though
I must admit that
occasionally I wouldn't mind
playing on their team,
just to get the inside scoop
on their moves.

Last week
I was his girlfriend—
always and forever.
Like an army,
he invaded my mind,
my heart.

I belonged to him—
not to my parents
nor even to myself.

How can something
that felt so good
change so quickly?
Like a warm pool
into ice.

When I thaw out
will I,
should I,
trust a boy again
with so much of whom I am?

I want to love.
I want to be loved.
Maybe as I grow older,
falling in love will become easier.

When I climb
in bed at night
and turn the lights out
on the world,
it's just You and me, God.

The rest of the people
who tell me who I am
may walk through my dreams,
but really
they're all
on the other side
of the closed door
of my eyelids.

Now, in the dark,
I can tell You who
I most want to be:
Your special daughter,
one You pick up
in Your arms
and let safely
sleep.

Growing up isn't easy, God;
It's just too soon for me to know
Just who the real me will be,
But with You there to guide me
I somehow think it's going to be fun.

And all my tomorrows?
Only You know,
but I trust You —
that You'll help me
build the days and years
on the foundation
we are slowly, carefully
mortaring in place,
slowly, carefully
cementing with grace.

Designed by Mary Tara O'Keefe